I0390414

With thanks to all my clients for providing the material for this great book.

Mark

Written in collaboration with Write Business Results. Contact writer Georgia Kirke to discuss your business book or copywriting requirements: **info@writebusinessresults.com**

Design and illustrations by Scarletta Design. See more of designer Jess Olorenshaw's work and get in touch at **www.scarlettadesign.com**

Mark Bradley is a financial adviser with True Potential Wealth Management LLP which is authorised and regulated by the Financial Conduct Authority. FRS Number 529810. Registered Head Office: Newburn House, Gateway West, Newburn Riverside, Newcastle upon Tyne, NE15 8NX. True Potential Wealth Management is a Limited Liability Partnership. OC356611.

Contents

Introduction

A new client came to see me earlier this year for no other reason than because his accountant had put us in touch, telling him he needed to reassess his pension. The client is an entrepreneur, a very successful one at that, and through mistrust and fear, had been putting a standard £200 per month into his pension since he could remember. His circumstances had changed drastically since he'd begun this contribution and not only could he afford to do significantly more, but he was missing out on all sorts of benefits that could improve the quality of life he was currently enjoying.

I thought about this very hard, because although I can completely understand how fear can hold people back - we all experience it - to me it seemed odd that an entrepreneur, a professional problem-solver and risk-taker, could have allowed it to stop him from growing that pot of money. Over the course of our conversation, I found out that the fear was really stemming from a notion he had that retirement was synonymous with stopping. So in his mind, putting his money into a pot that may or may not serve him in retirement felt like too big a risk to take and he hadn't calculated that risk because he didn't have a plan.

We talked through automation and savings strategies, I showed him how to use my firm's iPad app to track his money, and we talked about what he really wanted in his future and for now, and used that vision to create a plan that motivates and frees him, both mentally and financially. By the end of the meeting, he admitted that he'd suspected for years he needed an approach like this, but didn't think it was so easy and had buried his head in the sand having over-thought the whole thing. All he wanted was to retire free.

I often think of this client and tell this story when meeting others for three reasons. Firstly because it is the position of a lot of people, including highly successful people; more than who care to admit it. Secondly, because it was during this meeting that I realised more than ever that as a Financial Adviser, it is my role and responsibility to simplify retirement as much as possible for the people I work with. Thirdly, this story is important because it is so telling of a particular mindset of avoidance and regret that is severely limiting to it's sufferers and once addressed and eliminated, will immediately free the afflicted and transform fear of retirement into excitement, positivity and fun.

Whilst the book is aimed at, and I refer to entrepreneurs and business owners, the principles apply to everybody. Tax rules constrain us all, and I have not yet met a client who doesn't want an excellent, no-hassle service, regular updates and minimal paperwork, without spending a fortune on fees.

Whether you're an entrepreneur or a Finance Director, this book speaks directly to you. We're all in business to make a profit, and it's when we turn our business into a success that all the fun starts. My years of experience working with many others in your positions have taught me the benefit of common sense and simplicity. As a result, I base my solution around these 3 Common Sense Principles:

1. **Get automated**
2. **Pay yourself first**
3. **Regular review**

As these form the backbone of your retirement plan, I'll walk you through these strategies in more detail in Chapters 3 and 4, because they will form the backbone of your retirement plan. First, we're going to go into more depth on the changing face of retirement, and get focussed on your future.

While a lot will be covered, you may be relieved to know that this book's designed to be read in 90 minutes. This book gives you an indication of how to start thinking about a retirement plan. It's based on common sense and years of experience. If you take the blueprint in this book to heart, you'll have a simplified plan that excites and motivates you by the time you've finished reading.

Chapter 1
The Retirement Revolution

When I ask my clients, "What do you think of when you hear the word 'retirement?'", gardening, old age and funerals are some of the most common responses. I was listening to an 'I Love Marketing' podcast recently, and Dan Sullivan and Joe Polish were talking about life plans and preparing your business should the worst happen. The points they made were very profound. They noted that the makeup of most people's lives is like a coin. The whole coin is 100% of their lives. One side is 50%, which is often spent avoiding things, and the other side is also 50%, which is made up of regrets. Their entire lives are spent avoiding or regretting, and what they avoided are all the things they're now regretting.

The question is, what would you attempt to do if you knew you could not fail? People avoid and regret so many things, so let's put an entrepreneurial spin on the retirement conversation and see the awareness and motivation that comes as a result.

The first step is to review our definition of retirement. If you Google 'retirement', some of the first words you see are, 'giving up', 'withdraw', 'ceasing' and 'seclusion'. Nowhere can you find an accurate description of the possibilities of modern retirement. If we were choosing a word today for what life looks like as we hit our mid-60s, 70s and 80s, it seems unlikely that we'd land on, 'retirement'. While these years bring with them many changes, for a growing number of people, this time of life is about anything but withdrawal or retreat.

All around us there are millions of the most creative, productive and entrepreneurial workers. People who have amassed incredible expertise and talents over decades, and then we 'retire' them, along with all that accumulated talent, expertise and potential. The way we think and talk about retirement needs to catch up with what is already happening. The time has come to retire the old definition of retirement. A thriving retirement is, of course, greatly aided by financial security. It means realising that retirement can be a time of expansion, engagement and adventure.

But how do we get there? The truth is, we all know that in order to be wealthy and live the life we want there's more we could be doing - like saving more, spending less and making healthier lifestyle choices. There is no end of advice and 'secrets' to success out there already, so the chances are, you have heard a lot of it before. As you're reading this book, you may not have acted on it. Whether that's because you don't agree with it, or you're simply not implementing it, the truth is, we all know there's more we could be doing, but we don't do it. Why? There are obstacles.

What I've learned over years of working with entrepreneurs is that one of the biggest obstacles is complexity. Whether it's self-generated complexity or information overload, we now live in a digital age that means we're bombarded with a tonne of information every day, and this information can be confusing. The key, which this book will help you with, is to simplify and to use technology to your advantage. That may not sound easy, but I assure you that armed with a tactical approach such as the one outlined here, it can be.

It's important to note that this is not another book about money. It's a book about simplification. In the next 90 minutes, I will give you a blueprint for your lifetime wealth strategy that your Financial Adviser can implement for you.

~

We now live in a revolutionised world; one that is very different to the world we knew when we first started out in our careers, and it continues to change rapidly. New technologies are being created every day, quicker than most of us can keep up with. We receive conflicted messages that play on our emotions yet we're still expected to make sound financial decisions and plan appropriately.

Information overload and our fast-moving society can feel chaotic and hard to get a handle on even for the most seasoned risk-takers. As entrepreneurs, we will all have had periods of crisis and chaos. As much as we want to combat and tame it, in fact it's in our nature to create more. We can easily fall victim to 'analysis-paralysis', where we're faced with so many options we end up not making a decision either way, or conversely, making a snap decision based on what's best for us now, rather than what's best for us in the future.

That's why, in order to make good choices for your retirement, you need to take a step back from all the white noise and ask yourself what you really want first. We're going to explore this together in more detail shortly, and go through how you can leverage technology to simplify your retirement plan. But first, I'm going to let you in on the finance industry's biggest secret.

If someone were to ask you why you haven't implemented everything you know about money and retirement, why you haven't put a proper plan in place, why you sometimes make unhealthy lifestyle choices, your likely response would be an array of impossible-to-overcome obstacles, right? Well, here's the secret. They're not obstacles. They're myths. So, before we get started, I want to address those myths and let you in on the realities.

1. Myth: Retirement planning is all about making cut backs.

Reality: Maybe that's true if don't have too much money or are not in control of your income. But for a successful entrepreneur who lives and works for freedom, it's about the 3 Common Sense Principles. A successful retirement plan is one that takes away complexity, not freedom!

2. Myth: I'm not 'ready' to plan for retirement. It feels confusing - I'll get round to it later.

Reality: You already have all the resources you need to get what you want. Regardless of how much more you earn in between now and retirement, no matter how big your company grows, your mindset and attitude is what determines your retirement success, just as it does in business and in life. In waiting, you're simply denying yourself freedom in years to come.

3. Myth: Advisers/Insurance companies are out for themselves and can't be trusted.

Reality: There are so many Financial Advisers out there today that it can be hard to see the wood from the trees. However, when planning for your retirement, having the right adviser can be a key component. Unless you're well versed in pensions already, the chances are you won't immediately understand the financial jargon, and you shouldn't feel bad about that. You're not supposed to! We are. Choose an Adviser who speaks your language, who you can build a relationship with, and know that it's always OK to seek a second opinion. A good Adviser will give you easy access to your pension and empower you to review it and make changes without difficulty.

4. Myth: I don't 'get' technology.

Reality: Technology is much simpler than it used to be. It's now commonplace for people of all ages to use iPhones and iPads. In fact, I have clients in their 70's regularly checking their pension performance on their iPads using 4G connections, because they don't have Wifi! If you don't know how to use an iPad, it will take you just minutes to learn. The company I work with, for example, have software specifically designed so that you can track your pension and top up at the touch of a button. Anyone can use it, and you'll be shown how in your first meeting.

5. Myth: I've left it too late, it's probably not worth bothering.

Reality: It is never too late to start a pension plan. Yes, the later you leave it, the less leverage you have, depending on your financial situation of course, but on the whole there are always things you can be doing now that will benefit you later. Remember, it's not about making drastic changes and cutbacks, it's about simplifying life so that you can enjoy life now *and* later on.

Since the changes in pension rules in April 2015, it's all changed for pension savers. The retirement reforms give you many more flexible ways of saving for and spending your retirement fund. The options are varied and it requires good advice to take advantage of them. This benefits entrepreneurial thinkers like you. You can now choose what you do with that money in order to benefit from entrepreneurial freedoms of time, money, relationship, and purpose.

You are more in control than ever before of your retirement, your plan, your quality of life, what happens to your money once it's in a fund, and how actively involved in its progress you are, whether you choose to work with an Adviser or not. These changes support an entrepreneurial way of life, because you don't have to fit the old model of working really hard, putting loads into your pension, then stopping at 65 and just living off it.

The main driver behind all entrepreneurial business decisions is growth, whether that means growth of time or money, or having a bigger impact on those you work with. So if you don't like the sound of stopping at retiring, and you want a more creative, fun and fulfilling retirement, it is possible and I'm going to show you how.

If you plan on continuing to work on exciting projects and investments in later life, you may want to take advantage of these reforms and look at the best way to utilise your retirement pot. This is why there is a need for better money management and professional financial advice.

We know that humans are biased towards the present and often overlook future costs in favour of benefits now, so it's my aim to provide you with a tried, tested and true framework within which you can think about your retirement and create a relevant plan. It's great that we can now live the life we want, but we do need to exercise some responsibility and diligence so that we don't trip ourselves up down the line.

In reading this book, I hope you will see that there is now a revolutionary way of thinking of retirement; an entrepreneurial approach that focusses on your freedom rather than trying to reign you in, and enables you and your family to view your retirement as the next chapter, not the end of the road.

Chapter 2
The Future Focuser

It's important to understand that the strategies that got you to where you are today, are not going to be the same strategies that get you to where you want to be. When it comes to retirement, a future-focussed approach, while psychologically more difficult than a present-based one, will provide you with a more exciting life.

Given that we're used to answering only to ourselves, why is it so hard to make decisions that please the future you as well as the present you? We all know we should plan, eat well, sleep more, exercise, meditate, save, but most of the time we just don't. I'm certainly not here to make anyone feel guilty, although accountability and good habits do play a big part. Maybe it's because in order to reach your current level, you've had to be reactive and spin many plates, therefore planning ahead hasn't been on your radar. Maybe balancing family life with your business is challenging, so exercise pays the price. Maybe one of the myths above had you in its grips. Whatever your reason, you need to know that you can still have the retirement you want if you focus on the 3 Common Sense Principles.

Before we can become truly future-focussed though, it's important we "retire our definition of retirement", as Arianna Huffington cleverly put it, and start using language that more accurately describes modern retirement. Too many people think of retirement as either "the end", "the final act", or "game over" which is, frankly, depressing! For some people that may be the case; they work hard every day of their lives until they hit 60 or 65 years old then hang up their coat and look forward to long days of pottering around in the garden. For highly driven individuals, that's rarely the case.

Sometimes people are so acutely aware of this, they go to the other extreme and see retirement as some kind of new world, feeling pressure to suddenly fulfil their life purpose just because they're not in full-time work any more. They gear themselves up for retirement as if it's their biggest challenge yet, and reel off long bucket lists but because they're also worried about getting old, they give themselves unrealistic timeframes in which to achieve said list. You might be one of these people, or at least know someone else who describes retirement more like a "transformation", a "metamorphosis" as if they're waiting to hatch out of their cocoon and fly.

Thankfully the reality of an entrepreneurial retirement is a lot less intimidating, and a lot more holistic. Just as the business world is now leaning away from thinking of work as separate to home, just as you hear people talk about a work-life balance less and less, well-being in retirement just as in business is now focussed more on productivity and energy, and how we create and maintain it. Your professional, personal, and company achievements and progression all centre around you. They're all parts of one big whole, rather than isolated sections of life. We now understand more than ever that we are the creative force in our lives and in order to have the right amount of energy for all the various parts to make them a success, keeping us feeling like the best version of ourselves and providing for our families, there are various things that we can do.

We can only focus on the things we love doing, eliminate or minimise energy drains as much as possible, choose who we spend our time with carefully, keep ourselves confident and sharp through physical exercise and meditation, take time away from our businesses to recharge and rejuvenate, refill our creative cups by spending time on our hobbies and personal interests, surrounding ourselves with loving, supportive and accepting people. While these sound like distractions (because who has time for exercise and meditation when you've got a business to run? Can't you just catch up on sleep in retirement?!), this is actually good news. It means that we already have all the resources we need to set us up for the retirement we want. We don't have to reinvent the wheel, or make retirement as complex as rocket science.

We simply need to apply the same principles that serve us well in business, lifetime habits as well. In doing so, we will thrive in retirement just as we have done so far in the rest of our lives. In other words, a successful, meaningful, purposeful retirement hinges on what we put into it. We reap what we sow. That said, the 'Do It Yourself' retirement model only works for a small percentage of the population, as we've discussed. Partly because people with no investment expertise can't be expected to make the same financial decisions as qualified, experienced financial advisers, and also because with no end goal and no overview of what your retirement looks like, you may feel like you don't know what you're really aiming for. Without that purpose and without attaching our actions to a positive reward, the preparation can feel pointless.

This is why the top decision you can make now that will benefit you in retirement is to make a clear, concise plan. Your plan doesn't need to be overly detailed if you find that stressful, it doesn't need to be tedious at all. In fact, it should be the total opposite. Your retirement plan, which we'll look at in more detail in the next chapter, should be designed to motivate you, excite you and give you a sense of purpose. It should spur you on to make decisions now that feed into it. Think of your retirement plan as the colour within the lines. It's your vision, and you are the artist. You can choose the colours you use, you can make your picture as abstract, realist or three-dimensional as you like, and you can add to it or change it as you please. The role of the Financial Adviser in this analogy is to draw the lines in the first place according to your specifications, so that your vision has shape and structure.

To explore this concept further, consider when the last time was that you heard retirement explained in such an exciting, refreshing way. Have you ever? This is because retirement is always discussed in financial terms and associated with dying, not living. It's great there is now more flexibility, but we need to realise that our own well-being and ability to have the retirement we want depends on a similar transactional approach. It is not just financial bank accounts that require deposits in order to make withdrawals. Our emotional, spiritual, physical and mental accounts work the same way. We can't just withdraw all the time and not fill them back up. Without regular deposits before making withdrawals, your pot, be it financial, emotional, spiritual, mental or physical, will diminish. Nor can we always deposit and not withdraw, because doing things, challenging ourselves, taking on new commitments in order to gain new capabilities is how we get increased energy, creativity and success.

Think about this in terms of your relationships with others. We're all in business, so using a sales analogy, would you dream of asking a prospective customer for their time and their money before first giving them a good reason? Or if you're a Finance Director, would you write an extra £10,000 into the budget for the year for courses and accreditations without first putting forward a business case to the Owner outlining what the company stands to gain? You're successful so presumably you would not. Professionally, we are all in the business of creating value. We give something the other person needs and wants before claiming our reward. We deposit in the relationship bank before we make a withdrawal. If you do the same for yourself, you will thrive.

There are 3 classic approaches to retirement that stop us from doing this. Some people think that if they spend their working lives amassing as many savings as possible and putting them into a pension account somewhere, not to be touched until retirement, they'll be fine. Others think that when they retire, it'll be game over anyway and once they die, they're not so bothered if their businesses cease too and they don't want to spend their lives working so hard and saving, and not reaping any reward now, so why put so much effort into a plan? The third is that people feel that retirement is so far in the future, they don't give it too much thought and just assume they'll be fine. There is one fundamental problem with all of these approaches.

They don't take into consideration what you want. They don't allow you to say, "I want to do meaningful work, travel, and enjoy time with my children, and in later years, grandchildren". There is no plan, just blind, hard work with no guarantees. As driven individuals who work so hard for the very freedom this approach denies, it just doesn't make sense to allow that to happen. You want your hard work now to pay you now and later, and the only way to ensure that is to be in control and call the shots.

This is exactly why the financial part of your retirement plan should be one of the most straightforward parts. If you work with an Adviser you can trust, who empowers you to make holistic decisions with your best interests at heart, and who keeps it simple for you, you are free to make regular withdrawals and deposits from your other life accounts, knowing your money is being kept safe and secure by a qualified professional. This area of focus is what's truly exciting about retirement. All the research shows that increasing numbers of people don't want to just give up after a certain age. They want to embrace retirement as a fresh opportunity to explore new activities, make a bigger social contribution, learn, travel and explore, and this is something I'm seeing everyday in my own business.

Chapter 3
Your Journey

Part I: Where am I at?

One question I'm commonly asked by entrepreneurs and Directors is, "how do I make a robust plan for the next 25/35/45 years? I don't even know what'll be happening five years from now, and so much could have changed by then!" Let's make this real and actually start putting together your own future plan based on all the things you want. You'll soon see it's a lot easier than you may think!

First of all, let's look at where you are at now. Typically, when I meet new clients for the first time, they can identify with one of the following five scenarios when I ask them if they already have a pension in place. Circle which of the following apply to you:

Scenario 1: I started a pension then stopped. I have a number of plans that all seem like a good idea in my mind, at least when I took them out!

Scenario 2: I have no idea what I'm doing with my pension or where I'm at.

Scenario 3: I'm totally confused by pensions - there's so much paperwork!

Scenario 4: I have no pension, no goal and no proper plan.

Scenario 5: I've been working with a financial planner, but I'm seeking a second opinion.

The good news is that no matter which one of those you've circled, you've made your first significant step towards a free retirement. Particularly if your answer is 1-4, you've also been very brave. Many people feel guilty that they haven't done more up until now and that guilt encourages them to avoid the situation. In identifying where you are now, you have just set the trajectory for your retirement plan and minimised your chance of regrets in later life.

Throughout this book, you'll learn of ways in which technology can be easily leveraged to totally transform scenarios 1-4. You'll be amazed at how quickly these scenarios, which can have successful, smart business people in their grips for years, sometimes decades, can be eliminated. These feelings and fears that have led you to this point are about to disappear, and be replaced by knowledge and tools that if acted on, have the power to change your life. If you circled Scenario 5, I'll just share a story with you.

A friend once told me about a friend of his (John), who had been going to his trusted optician for 10 years. They knew each other fairly well as you can imagine. Each year, John was fitted and supplied with a new pair of glasses for his short-sightedness. In the 11th year, he decided to seek another opinion from another optician, almost on a whim. He just thought he should probably try someone new as it had been so long. The new optician told him he actually had cataracts and probably didn't need glasses at all. That second opinion could have saved John's sight. For you, seeking a second opinion from another Financial Adviser may just confirm that you're already doing all the right things and you have the right Adviser, but it's rarely a waste of time.

The next step is an audit. This is the part most people find the most painful and if your outgoings haven't been seriously looked at for a while, years perhaps, the bulk of an audit might not be fun. It can, however, be cathartic. So, if you think you're going to feel cross with yourself or guilty, I encourage you to rip off the plaster and just do it. That psychological sense of relief once it's complete will feel so good! An audit could, and should, be really straightforward. The aim is to create a snapshot of where your money's going over time, so you can use facts to make better spending decisions. It doesn't have to be complicated or a big commitment. To demonstrate just how simple this can be, I suggest keeping a daily record of your spending over a short period time. The 'One Week Challenge' is ideal. Simply record how much you spend and what on for seven days. See page 25 for a simple One Week Challenge template.

This exercise isn't supposed to be tedious, it's simply there to give you a birdseye view of what goes out and what you could accumulate. The business owner is no different to anyone else. The more you earn the more you spend. The difference for entrepreneurs is that money equals freedom. It's one of the reasons you became an entrepreneur in the first place, which is why impulse spending works against you more than others. Watching the small stuff is important because if accumulated, it can turn into life-changing amounts of money, which could significantly increase your freedom. I bet you earn more than you did 10 years ago, but have you got more wealth? Do the challenge, and just be aware of that spending and think about what that could mean for you if it were allowed to accumulate over 5, 10 or 20 years. Let's see if we can turn your impulse spending into impulse saving! There'll be more on this in Chapter 4.

One Week Challenge Template

Monday		Tuesday		Wednesday		Thursday		Friday		Saturday		Sunday	
Item	Amount £/p	Item	Amount £/p	Item	Amount £/p	Item	Amount £/p	Item	Amount £/p	Item	Amount £/p	Item	Amount £/p

Now you know where all that hard-earned cash is going, let's explore what you'd like to happen in your retirement if money wasn't the main obstacle. Again, this can be a really straightforward exercise, and when thinking about your future, really open yourself up to all kinds of options and possibilities. Here are some questions to get you started if this is difficult:

- What needs to happen for you to feel happy with your retirement? i.e. working 4 days per week on projects that excite you, taking 6 weeks a year off, travelling to dream destinations.

- At what age do you think you're going to die? How would you like to be feeling at that point? What sort of things would you like to be doing when the time comes? Who do you want around you?

- What would you like to be known for?

- Write down your age and/or the age at which you plan on retiring, and subtract it from the age you think you're going to die at. This is the number of years you have to carve a whole new chapter of life for yourself if you so wish. If there were no obstacles, how would you spend those years?

- Think about things you do or have done in your past that give you so much energy and buzz that they get you out of bed in the morning. The activities, hobbies and personality traits that, when you're doing them, feel so amazing, free and natural that you may not even realise you're brilliant at them. Those things that others love in you, and when you're in that zone, you notice friends, colleagues, family and strangers tend to want to be around you. Out of everything you do and have ever done, what are the top three things that you love the most?

- What are the things you wish you could do if nothing got in your way? The bucket list items that you yearn for deep down but life seems to have a habit of making something else more urgent always comes up?

Out of everything you've written down, what are the top 5 things you'd like to make happen the most. The things that if you were to focus purely on those and everything else was taken away, would make you the happiest you possibly can be.

1.
2.
3.
4.
5.

Now that you've brainstormed how you'd like to spend your retirement, take a few minutes to write out what you'd like to happen in between now and the point of your retirement. How would you like to advance all the different areas of your life? Imagine and daydream future scenarios and let that vision flow onto paper and write it out like a narrative, in the first person, as if you're at that future point now. Consider all aspects of your life; where do you see yourself personally, professionally, with your team if you have one, family, friends, partner, health, wellbeing?

Out of all the things you've written down, choose the top 3 areas of focus. Just like before, if everything were taken away from you and you could only have 3 things back, what would they be?

1.
2.
3.

Why are these so important?

What are the obstacles, if any, that could prevent you from getting what you want in these 3 areas?

What are some of the top strategies that could help you overcome those obstacles and move you towards your retirement?

Write down the first actions you can take today to progress each area:

You've now got a good enough overview of what you're currently spending, you know what your income is, you've brainstormed and shortlisted all the things you'd like to do in your retirement, you've identified the top areas you need to focus on now, and you know how you're going to progress those areas so that you're in the best place you can be to pursue the retirement of your dreams. Not bad for a few minutes' work!

Part III - Making it happen

Now you know what you want, we can get down to the nitty gritty - the numbers. Let's not kid ourselves here, not many of us are fans of budgets and budgeting. It's boring stuff and as you've just discovered, you're not planning on living a boring life! It's reasonable to suggest therefore that a plan centred around saving via a budget is destined to fail, so let's take a different approach. This is where the 3 Common Sense Principles come in:

1.   Get automated

Make investing in your retirement a one-time decision. What I mean by that is, we need to create a plan for you that once set up and agreed, allows life to go on. The plan is executed automatically, with little or no manual input from you. All you need to do is decide what you want. We're all familiar with the line, "the best laid plans of mice and men often go awry", so the reason I suggest you work with an Adviser when you've just done all that thinking and brainstorming, is because plans change and you don't want to go through all that leg work from scratch. For example, what if you live longer than you thought you would? Or God forbid, the opposite happens and you find out you've got less time than you wanted? Having an expert in your corner who fully understands your goals and motivations who will be able to guide you and help you restructure your plan in the event of sudden change. You may also have general questions from time to time.

The software I use with my clients is fantastic because it allows you to input goals and track their progress, whilst getting them to concentrate on the activities that are most important.

2.   Pay yourself first

Every time you earn a pound, pay yourself first, preferably before tax. Most people go about it wrong. They earn money to pay overheads and bills. They pay themselves a wage or dividends from the business. They then pay tax on drawings and corporation tax on what's left. Then, they leave money inside the business for later. Of course, cash flow is fundamental. So let's ask ourselves, what will we sell the business for? Profit x 1, profit x 2? I hear business owners say, "my business is my retirement fund", so why not pay yourself with funds that have not been taxed. You are ultimately your best investment.

Here's how it works: £1,000 gets a corporation tax deduction of 20%, so for every £800 there's £200 tax relief, giving a 25% return. Simple! The decision is how much to start with; 5%, 10%, 20% of your income? This is something we can work out together, using the information in Part I, and look to increase over time. Once we know that number, we automate it. Remember you'll also benefit from compound interest. Just as the Nike slogan says, "Just Do It", with this method it's more like, "Just Do It Once". This is what I've done with my own pension, and it works.

3.   Review

Once you're set up, review your pension to stay in control. Again, this should be really simple and straightforward. Use technology to help you record, retain and track the retirement plan you create. I use my firm's technology platform because it's user-friendly, you can use it to track your saving and spending 24/7 on your iPad, and you can make changes quickly and easily. It's also smart, because it looks at your finances as a whole and helps you set multiple goals, whilst keeping your investments working together.

A lot of people don't realise they can use technology to simplify their retirement. But, if you think about it, back in our parents' day, before the web, mobile and tablets, everyone had their black book of expenses and earnings. The iPad is your modern day black book that you can carry around with you and add to whenever you want or need. Using it with specially designed software is infinitely more efficient of course, because it's not just a record, it's a constantly active database that moves with you and your goals.

You need technology that can do this in order to keep your plan really simple, because whether it's saving for a new car, the trip of your dreams a few years from today or investing for your retirement, all your goals work together. Like any journey, if you want to reach your destination, you need to know how much you have in the tank to ensure you can make it. Of course, things can then change along the way, so as the goalposts move, you can simply adjust your plan, save a lump sum impulsively for example, and update it whenever you want. It's that flexible.

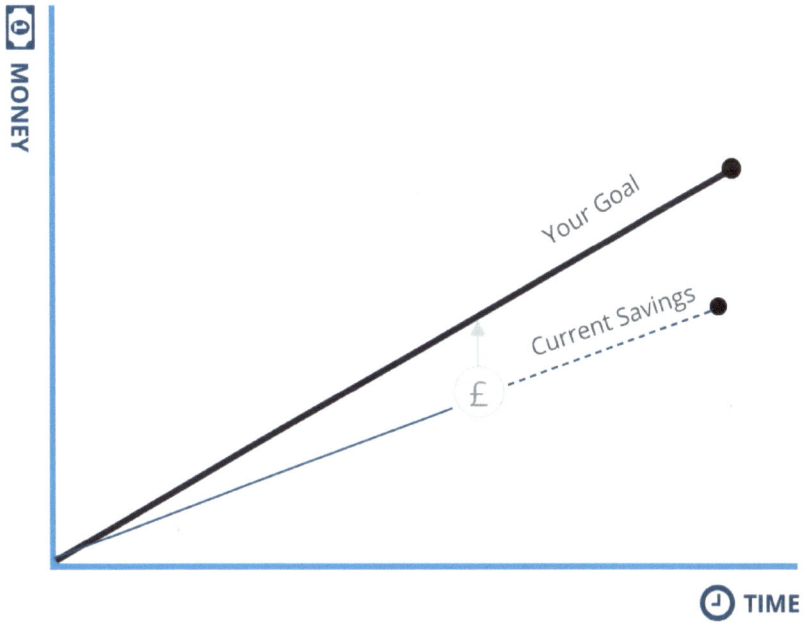

The plan and the decision is always the hardest part, not because creating a plan is hard, but because as we've discussed already, our minds make up obstacles and we're often so focussed on the short- and mid-term that the future's hard to consider in detail. You've now done the hard bit, and we haven't even met yet. The information that you've written down and digested since picking up this book is invaluable. While it may need some refining and further discussion, you have just created the supporting structure for the rest of your life.

Remember the entrepreneur who'd avoided his pension for years because it was too much to think through on his own? That's no longer you. You've already transformed your future just by thinking about it, writing it down and getting clear on it. This is why I'm writing this book and sharing all this information with you. There's no need for you to go through this process on your own, and in fact, you shouldn't have to. It's so much easier and simpler when you make that shift from thinking you'll get round to doing it at some point to committing to taking action today and letting someone help you.

That said, all of this preparation is worth nothing without action, and the next step is for you to commit to making your plans a reality.

Chapter 4
Technology & Tactics

As a partner with one of the UK's leading financial services providers, I work with professionals and business owners to help them achieve their business goals. We deal with all wealth issues; cash extraction from the business via pensions, ISA and personal investment portfolios. Over the course of the last 30 years working in the financial services industry in London and the Midlands, and as a member of the Personal Finance Society and a Chartered Insurance practitioner, one thing I've learnt and want you to take away from this book is how easy it can be for you to achieve your financial goals. It doesn't have to be rocket science or stressful, and embracing technology can significantly simplify your personal and professional lives.

I am a great advocate of technology because I can use it to deliver a unique service that ticks all the boxes; all investments are in one place, there's no paper, everything's valued automatically, your plan and its execution can be automated and you can be in full control from your smartphone, iPad or desktop. There's a minute margin for error and it's so efficient. Technology to me has become part of the unique teamwork within my business. It certainly hasn't replaced anyone, but it supports me in my areas of focus and my future because it helps to take care of the most important part of my business; you.

This is why I strongly recommend embracing technology. I know and feel the benefits first hand, and it works for everyone. Earlier I mentioned my client in his 70s who accesses his iPad once a day to check on his portfolio. He wasn't connected to the internet before I set him up. Whilst on an Alaskan cruise myself, I noticed that the ship had an iLounge and a daily seminar on hints and tips on how to use technology to simplify your life. It was full every day with people of all ages, many in their 60s and 70s.

Leveraging technology is the ideal way to set and monitor goals, whilst leaving everything in order for the next generation. The modern little black book, the locked case in the loft labelled, "in the event of an emergency", technology keeps all your account numbers and names to contact safe in the case of death. My firm's app is incredibly easy to use; so much so it's used already by people with little or no computer experience.

~

In Chapter 1, I talked about how the 2015 pension reforms and the age of the entrepreneur have worked together to revolutionise retirement. The major opportunity for businesses in this market is cash extraction. Most businesses do not understand how positive the opportunities actually are. It is rare that if a company is making profits and sitting on cash, that I do not come out of a meeting where an entrepreneur has not decided to make monthly contributions of £2,000 - £3,000 or the maximum £40,000 single premium.

Something I see repeated time and time again is that most business owners limit what they take out of the business because they don't want to pay the tax. Income tax rates rise rapidly and dividend taxation is changing. Now is the time to get a proper handle on what we take out. In my practice, we look at maximising the tax efficient extraction of funds by using a pension. A better way of describing this is a tax efficient savings plan with a time lock to age 55. 25% tax free at 55 years old is extremely attractive.

We also utilise your spouse or partner's position, should you have one. Spouses are often employed within the business, so we use their pension allowance. Many entrepreneurs give their partner an allowance out of the business. The question is do you think this is going to continue in retirement? If so, where are the funds going to come from? The best thing to do is fund it now. One of the major advantages to the change in pension rules is that it's allowed us to be creative.

Many businesses sit on large cash deposits so they are not 'in hock' to the bank. These deposits then build up over a long period of time. Businesses worry about succession plans; I have one client that is now drawing from retirement funds whilst still working in the business. This allows the business to flourish without the strain of the owner's drawings. It's a great strategy for generational planning. I have another client who was once a high-flying business owner who is just over the state pension age. He draws his state pension then tops it up with tax-free cash, uses his annual capital gains tax allowance and draws from an extensive ISA portfolio. The result is that he is currently a non-taxpayer.

You have to have your eggs in the right baskets to be able to achieve this, so you can see how clever, common sense planning pays real dividends and easily pays for itself. The key to this is a good relationship with your Financial Adviser. One that's based on visibility and open communication as well as trust.

Chapter 5
Success Strategies Summary

_____

Retirement is revolutionised

- It's no longer about stopping, it's about being fulfilled
- Pensions have changed too, so you can be entrepreneurial in retirement as well as now
- A good Financial Adviser will always put you in control

Keep it simple

- Ask for help from a qualified, experienced Adviser you trust
- Apply The 3 Common Sense Principles
- Use technology

Planning is priceless

- Retirement isn't purely a financial matter
- It takes some time to begin with, but a plan that motivates you is essential
- Don't delay! You're only denying yourself the freedom you're working so hard to achieve

Don't let fear stop you

- Fear is the biggest reason some people never get what they want
- Make the choices now that will get you to where you want to be in 10 years' time

- Ask yourself, "what would I do if I knew I could not fail?"

Remembering this simple formula when thinking about your retirement will keep you on track and help you revolutionise your retirement:

MINDSET + TECHNOLOGY = ABUNDANCE

With over 30 years experience in the financial services sector, **Mark Bradley** understands the importance of putting clients first. A fan of using technology to simplify life and work, Mark has now shared his own innovative approach to retirement to help others achieve similar results. Applying the blueprint outlined in this book to his own life allows Mark to continually improve and tailor the solutions he presents to his clients.

For a more in depth conversation with Mark, call 0121 288 9331 or 0207 193 3686 to schedule your appointment, or email markbradley@tpllp.com

www.ingramcontent.com/pod-product-compliance
Lightning Source LLC
Chambersburg PA
CBHW041205180526
45172CB00006B/1202